Cind

a play

The Cast

- **Narrator**
- **Cinderella**
- **Stepmother**
- **Stepsister 1**
- **Stepsister 2**
- **Fairy Godmother**
- **Messenger**
- **Prince**
- **Guests at the dance**

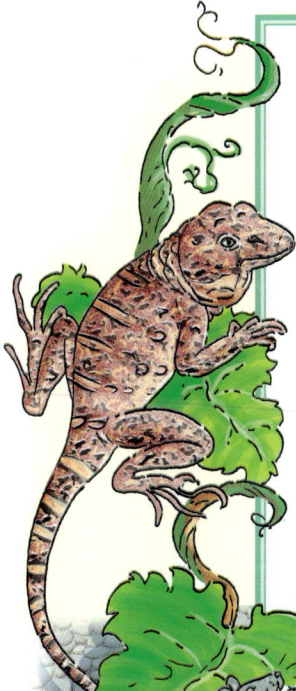

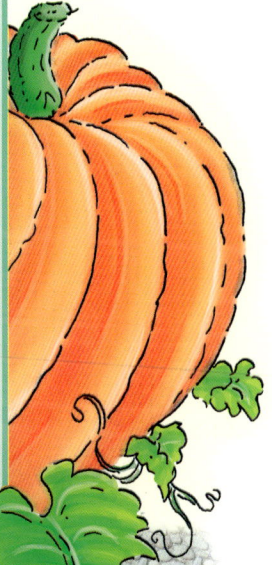

Retold by Brenda Parkes
Illustrated by Margaret Power and Martin Shepherd

Narrator	Once upon a time, a lovely girl with the name "Cinderella" lived with her stepmother and stepsisters. They were very lazy, and they treated Cinderella badly.
Stepmother	Cinderella! You have made our beds, haven't you?

Cinderella   They are almost ready.

Stepsister 1   Good! We need to have our morning nap.

Stepsister 2   And make our lunch! We'll want it when we wake up!

Narrator	One day, a messenger came to the door.
Messenger	There is to be a dance at the palace. The prince is inviting everyone.
Stepsisters	How exciting!
Stepmother	We must all get new dresses…
Stepsister 1	*and* new slippers!

Cinderella	May *I* go to the dance?
Stepsister 1	What could you *wear*?
Stepsister 2	And just look at your *hair*!
Stepmother	No! You may *not* go to the dance!

Narrator	On the night of the dance, Cinderella helped her stepsisters and stepmother to get ready. When they finally left, she sat and cried.
Cinderella	Oh, I wish that *I* could go to the dance!
Narrator	At that moment, a woman with a magic wand appeared.

Fairy Godmother	Don't cry, Cinderella. I'm your fairy godmother, and I'll help you get your wish. You *will* go to the dance!
Cinderella	Oh, thank you! But *how*?
Fairy Godmother	First, you must find me a big pumpkin, six mice, and a lizard.

Narrator After Cinderella had found all these things, her fairy godmother changed the pumpkin into a golden coach.

Cinderella How wonderful!

Fairy Godmother	I haven't finished yet!
Narrator	At that very moment, the six mice turned into six beautiful horses, and the lizard became a handsome driver.

Fairy Godmother	Now it's *your* turn, Cinderella.
Narrator	A moment later, Cinderella was wearing a beautiful dress and lovely glass slippers.
Cinderella	Oh, I feel like a princess!
Fairy Godmother	It's time to go, Cinderella. But remember: You must be home by 12 o'clock. That's when my magic will end.

Narrator	When Cinderella got to the dance, everyone started talking about her.
Guests	Who is that beautiful girl? What a lovely dress, and what amazing glass slippers! She must be a princess!

Prince	Will you dance with me please?
Cinderella	With pleasure!
Narrator	The prince and Cinderella danced together all evening.

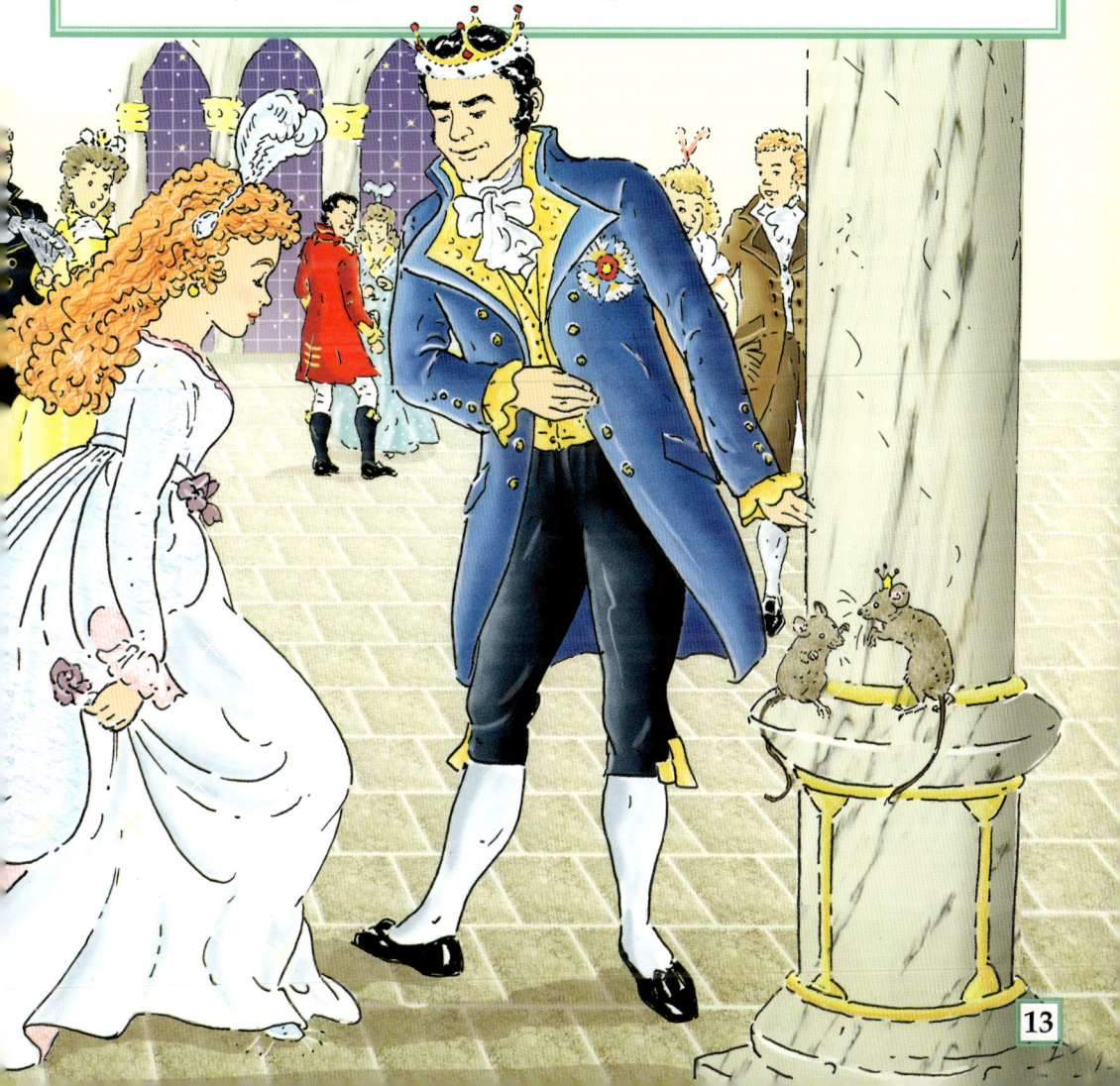

13

Stepsister 1 Just look at them dance!

Stepsister 2 When will *we* get a chance?

Narrator Then the clock began to strike twelve. Cinderella suddenly remembered what her fairy godmother had told her.

Cinderella	I must go!
Prince	Stop! Why are you running away? And look, one of your slippers has fallen off.

Narrator	But Cinderella could not stop. When she reached home, the magic had ended, but she still had one glass slipper.
Cinderella	I will keep it forever!

The prince had kept the other slipper.
He gave it to his messenger, and he sent him
to search everywhere for that beautiful girl.

Messenger   Did anyone from this house go to the dance at the palace?

Stepsisters   Yes, Yes! We were there!

Messenger   The prince has sent me to find someone very special. She wore this slipper to the dance.

Stepsister 1	Give it to me!
Stepsister 2	No! Let *me* try it first!
Narrator	The stepsisters pushed and pulled the slipper, but they could not make it fit.

Cinderella   Please, may *I* try?

Stepmother   Don't be stupid. You didn't go to the dance!

Messenger   That's OK. Let her try.

Narrator	Of course, the slipper fit perfectly.
Cinderella	I have the other slipper, too.
Stepsister 1	*What?*
Stepsister 2	*You?*
Stepmother	I don't believe it!

Narrator   When Cinderella put on the second slipper, the magic returned, and suddenly she was wearing the beautiful dress again.

Messenger Please come to the palace with me at once.
The prince will be very happy because
I have found you.

Soon Cinderella and the prince were married. They invited everyone to the wedding, and, of course, Princess Cinderella and the prince lived happily ever after.